I0059516

TAKE THE HOUSE

A Proposal to Reform the Republic

Matthew Wells Sanders

Copyright © 2017 Matthew Wells Sanders.

Brooke Saron was an editor, who did a wonderful job of content editing the
first draft of the manuscript, and I would like to acknowledge her.

All rights reserved. No part of this book may be reproduced, stored, or transmitted by any
means—whether auditory, graphic, mechanical, or electronic—without written permission
of the author, except in the case of brief excerpts used in critical articles and reviews.
Unauthorized reproduction of any part of this work is illegal and is punishable by law.

An American Patriot Enterprises
3 Monroe Parkway, Ste P-124 Lake Oswego, OR 97035

ISBN: 9780578187501 (sc)
ISBN: 9780578187518 (e)

Library of Congress Control Number: 2016920159

Because of the dynamic nature of the Internet, any web addresses or links contained in
this book may have changed since publication and may no longer be valid. The views
expressed in this work are solely those of the author and do not necessarily reflect the
views of the publisher, and the publisher hereby disclaims any responsibility for them.

Any people depicted in stock imagery provided by Thinkstock are models,
and such images are being used for illustrative purposes only.
Certain stock imagery © Thinkstock.

rev. date: 03/03/2017

Contents

Introduction

My fellow American, you are a fully vested owner in the American enterprise, and that claim to ownership has nothing to do with wealth, property holdings, or lineage.

Our current system of legislative representation in the United States of America is dysfunctional and broken. Accountability is nonexistent where it is most critical, undermining any basis of credibility in the current government, in business, in law enforcement, in the economy, and in claims of property and wealth transferred over the last several decades.

We, the American people at large, need to take control of our political system in order to establish our collective rights as owners of the American enterprise by securing irrevocable access to direct participation in the legislature. The idea is simple: if you don't have to sell your soul to legislate, you won't owe the devil anything when you do. If the legislature were composed of nearly every type of citizen, fair and equitable accountability would be effortless. The product of legislation would be the most efficient, ingenious, and harmonious laws one would naturally expect of a great and educated people! At the very least, our collective action (and chosen inaction) would reflect a more appropriately defined will of the people on a matter, showing mercy and restraint where due as well as a more energetic and exacting response on issues of human dignity.

At the same time, this body would enjoy an authority and mandate in full proportion to the people's proper faith in the functional abilities of the institution itself. In other words, if the people *in* the House of Representatives *are* us, we would respect that institution as much as we would naturally trust any group of us. The same principals and benefits attributed to the concept of a jury of our peers apply in this regard. Using the same principal at the top of the system as is used at the bottom to the same effect, in terms of overall quality control of the product of governance, is the solution.

This change will appeal to the Democrats, the Republicans, independents, big businesses, small businesses, the wealthy, and the poor alike. It is completely nonpartisan. This solution is required to avoid an instability and pervasive inequality that will continue to undermine the concepts on which America was founded. If we fail to take the appropriate actions as citizens united by our common cause, we will soon be forced to say, "Farewell to all thy greatness."

The current trends of technology, automation, adaptive algorithms, and applied artificial intelligence will offer challenges to governance and to our economic models that our current electoral process will be incapable of addressing or defending itself and its populace from. We the people need to take control of our House of Representatives with the following amendment to the Constitution of the United States.

The "Take the House" Amendment

The House of Representatives shall be composed of members chosen by random lottery of all eligible citizens who have volunteered for the selection pool.

Every second year, the people of the states will vote to retain or dismiss their representatives on an individual basis. Upon a vote of dismissal or a vacancy, a new lottery will be immediately held.

No person shall be a representative who has not attained to the age of twenty-five years, has not been seven years a citizen of the United States, has not passed the naturalization civics test as required of naturalized citizens by law, or will not, when elected, be an inhabitant of that congressional district in which he or she shall be chosen.

The time has come, once again, for the people of our nation to take a full appraisal of our collective experience and our system of government, and to reform our system of government to embody more closely the ideals espoused by our founding fathers and the many faithful patriots who have followed.

Fortunately, Americans are a people of startlingly effective action. When Americans do start to see clearly and collaboratively identify a solution that is not worse than the current disease, they will quickly become united. It is in this spirit that I offer a framing of the core issues affecting us, a comprehensive solution, and a pragmatic approach to implementation. I'm ever grateful that we have the opportunity, ability, and duty to continue the great journey and tradition gifted to us by our predecessors.

I leave you with an excerpt from the first of *The Federalist Papers*, written to the colonists to explain the need to form a stable and effective government, noting that they were embarking on an experiment on which the world would judge them. We stand on firm foundations due to their boldness, foresight, and ability to reason with and consequently trust one another. Although time has passed, the challenge to us and its natural implication remain the same.

> AFTER an unequivocal experience of the inefficiency of the subsisting federal government, you are called upon to deliberate on a new Constitution for the United States of America. The subject speaks its own importance; comprehending in its consequences nothing less than the existence of the UNION, the safety and welfare of the parts of which it is composed, the fate of an empire in many respects the most interesting in the world. It has been frequently remarked that it seems to have been reserved to the people of this country, by their conduct and example, to decide the important question, whether societies of men are really capable or not of establishing good government from reflection and choice, or whether they are forever destined to depend for their political constitutions on accident and force. If there be any truth in the remark, the crisis at which we are arrived may with propriety be regarded as the era in which that decision is to be made; and a wrong election of the part we shall act may, in this view, deserve to be considered as the general misfortune of mankind.

The Structural Nature of the Problem

It seems that everyone knows there is a huge problem with our form of government, but few people seem to know precisely what to do about it. There is a sense that this is the way things have always been, and that there is no realistic way to improve the situation. More problematic is that no single fix seems to solve the fundamental issues that plague our republican form of government, and no one in authority is willing to provide meaningful accountability. However, we must note the following.

- **Most of the political problems we face as a nation should be expected, given the way our constitution prescribes how we choose the individuals who form our nation's laws and policies.** Currently, both members of the Senate and the House of Representatives are selected by popular vote, with enormous amounts of cash and access to media outlets needed to run their marketing campaigns.

- **Our constitution did not always select members of the Senate and the House of Representatives in the same manner.** Originally, selecting senators was left up to the states. This method, which allowed slavery to flourish in the republic since its inception, was not without its faults.

- **The reason for selecting the Senate and the House by different means was notably important to the early American colonists arguing for the formation of the republic, and those principals are crucial to the realization of a stable legislative branch.** The quintessentially different primary feature of the republic, compared

1

to a democracy, is that a few representatives of the populace make decisions on their behalf, rather than the populace en masse directly deciding all issues. The constitutional convention and the debate before and during gave much focus to how these representatives could be selected in a fair and reliable manner. Slavery compounded the issue, because states that depended upon the practice were concerned that a representation that tilted to the Northern point of view would impose a moral obligation that would threaten what Southern white men saw as their freedom to take away the freedoms of other human beings. Selecting members of the Senate was left up to the states. This meant that each state could appoint men who would ensure that the state's way of life could be maintained. The popular vote always decided the membership of the House of Representatives. The fewer number of senators and the greater number of House of Representatives members were calculated, the authors argued, to create the right-sized sample to properly distill the ideas from the populace to the representatives while being granular enough to illicit a full variety in points of view. Creating this atmosphere was seen as crucial to allowing the spread of ideas, culture, and economic opportunity among the various states to encourage a rich, interconnected society while also (theoretically) preventing popular or special-interest factions.

These two differently composed legislative bodies were able to successfully provide this kind of stability for the minority of white male landholders, until the nation as a whole was forced to face the fact that by denying entire classes of humanity the recognition of being human, we were denying them the protections we ourselves had sought from British rule. Shortly after the Civil War, Americans pointed out that the system of selecting representatives that had worked so effectively to promote and maintain the practice of slavery and human trafficking was obviously a corrupt mechanism that had no chance of offering a just and stable government at the federal level or any level. The Seventeenth Amendment was then adopted to ensure that senators were no longer appointed by the state governments but elected by popular vote. Corruption was the claim then, and it is the same now.

- **The changes prescribed in the Seventeenth Amendment to the constitution were beneficial and necessary for the socioeconomic and political problems facing our nation at the time, in order to prevent abuses by those holding power. Similar changes are again necessary in order to realize a government that pretends to be of, for, and by the people.** Obviously, regressing to the form of government that allowed actual slavery in all of its sick, perverted horror to function in this country is out of the question. Essentially, we already have a version of modern royalty trying to subjugate what they consider to be the rest of us poor, undeserving idiots. We shouldn't hand them the historical means by which individuals successfully kept similar power the last time—that would lead to our destruction, first by our own hands, and then by a world that wants to rid itself of our embarrassment. The rest of the world might miss the industry and trade we provide them, but they would judge the experiment of liberty and freedom a bitter mistake.

However, the concept that popular opinion and monetary influence is insufficient as a reliable mechanism by which to choose *all* representatives is hard truth. The founding fathers had a good reason for not designing the system with that singular selection mechanism! They were extremely suspicious of the influence that wealth and power, especially foreign power, might have on the legislative process. It is also interesting to note that, similarly to the historical events that took place leading up to and at the end of the Civil War, opinions changed about who is human and to what degree they now deserved the basic things one had always attributed as human rights.

We need to apply the same type of thinking that kept these two different bodies of the legislature *different in their natures* and that is seen elsewhere in similar governments that have a clear House of Lords and House of Commons type of composition. In the spirit of both progression and reform, the mix of electing senators and seeding the House of Representatives through random selection would give the healthiest balance to the legislature. The House of Representatives would be more beholden to the people, which *The*

Federalist Papers mention is the most effective deterrent to building a wall of separation between the office and the people.

Under the Take the House Amendment, each two-year cycle, the people would be able to focus solely on the job performance of the individual representative and his or her work history in Congress without confusing the issue with an alternative personality to vote for. This would prevent party politics from colluding to remove entire subjects like slavery, women's rights, and so on from the public debate. It would create a unique environment where we could effectively eliminate the ability to pay off a legislator, establishing a bedrock within government by which accountability could effectively take place.

- **The constitution of our republican form of democracy must also change if it will have any chance of standing the test of time.** We ourselves have put the rationality and integrity of our entire socioeconomic and political system in question due to a complete lack of accountability. Unfortunately, we are faced with the reality that corrupt justice ain't no justice at all. Any solution that focuses on mere legislation is insufficient to address the core issues. The offense has always been a limited view of who is considered a first-class citizen in this country. It is time, once again, to change the corporate bylaws to reflect the corporate charter. In doing so, we lay the foundation on which accountability can take place; legislation can be rendered with the full support and authority of the will of the people; and the values, needs, and real experiences of the many can serve as a constant basis of sanity in the discussion and debate process. Any other alternative, or even continuing with the same governmental mechanisms, invites the ruin that will certainly come when things are pushed to further extremes.

The tentative nature of any property claim, which was pointed out so clearly by our founding fathers when explaining to the colonists the necessity of establishing a federal government that could command authority on such matters to a world that questioned its right to exist, naturally comes into play when the sanity and soundness of our systems of justice are found to be lacking. If a people of any nation come to find that the scales of justice and the scales of the marketplace have been weighted, and those in the government have found it in their best interest to hold their fingers on the scales with predictable prejudice, we learn two things: (1) those groups experiencing the worst of the effects learn that trusting others and trusting their government is a mistake, and (2) everyone else learns that when the power shifts, the institution has no mechanism to prevent a reciprocal injustice on them.

It would be a grave mistake to attribute the failings of our current legislature to a failure of the overall structure and necessity of the republican form of government we have today. It would be a tragedy to assume its institutions are not fully capable of handling the tasks we require of them in a safe and efficient manner. However, if this atmosphere of corruption continues, I fear the public will throw the baby out with the bathwater in bitter disgust. I submit that the change I am suggesting is the same type of change enacted after the Civil War in order to fight a corrupt atmosphere of wealthy factions. I point this out for those who think it can never get that bad; it already has once. Some may think my change is too radical; it has already been done once. I am making the point so that I can hold us all to the following rational suggestion: long before we get to the next civil war, let's fix the problems inherent in our legislative branch selection process that are causing the issues that lead to war in the first place! There is nothing special, scary, or prophetic about calling for the exact change I am suggesting. We were told we would need to do these things, we have done them before as a people for the exact same reasons, and there has never been any illusion that this type of evolution and maintenance wouldn't be required in the future.

- **This is a problem that must be solved quickly, peacefully, soundly, and with full cooperation and commitment by both political parties and the American people at large.** There is too much at stake. In our current environment, the response of the two parties has been to pull further apart in ideology while the tone of the language used has become decidedly more threatening. We are, arguably, the most powerful geopolitical force on the planet, and for better or for worse, we are the standard-bearer for a free society. When the world sees us divided, they stand poised to take advantage of the situation. Ninety-nine percent of the American population rightly fears being decimated, and at this point in time, with nothing new injected into the public debate, they can count on the government to continue to render the same as it has for the last thirty years or so. I have mentioned my disdain for the failed thinking that would advocate for completely destroying the current system. The fact is, I can already see the media priming the population for it—and the population is about ready to try anything! Rumors have it that the next generation is already being tagged "the Founders" by a major media outlet. That's frightening to me because other than the idea I am presenting to you now, I have heard of no alternative plan for reformation. Someone is planning *something*, and that title requires a lot of explanation.

One of the main reasons I am anxious to get this idea out is because I don't think the American people will do nothing. The absence of any single real good solution will invite a horde of destructive ones—and several with deadly intent! I will make the bold case that some elements of party politics have been test-driving exactly how much of the population they can get to emotionally react to various issues to directly quantify to individuals which basic ideas of freedom they will freely toss aside in furious support of, or reaction to, the particular issue at hand. The fallacious concept of freedom of religion for all but Muslims is the clearest example to come to mind. If the current system remains, I calculate that it won't be hard, in the near future, to get the population of the United States to elect a set of people capable of making just about any decision regarding their future, no matter how far it deviates from what we recognize as a free society.

If anything, it can't be said that an answer hasn't been offered. I will be satisfied in knowing that at least this idea exists as a reasonable standard to compare other alternatives against! Certainly, this type of reform should be tried, once again, to see if we can garnish the same effect of growing and maturing together as a people, taking advantage of the bountiful future that unfolds as we each learn to maximize our individual potentials and enrich those around us through a productive participation in our communities!

- **The government must be reformed to reflect the reality that we are all owners in the American enterprise.** That state of ownership must be reflected in real guarantees of direct participation in the legislature. By naming all citizens as first-class crew by nature, we enshrine the concepts of civil rights and our united fate into functional reality, demanding the civil duties of joint preparedness, collaboration, understanding, and compromise as a more naturally obvious result. With our modern capabilities, we stand uniquely poised to take advantage of our ability to educate the populace toward this end. There is no argument compatible with our history, tradition, stated purpose, or continued evolution as a nation and peoples against educating the American people, compulsorily and en masse, to be fully capable of participating in the full duties of the legislature. Anyone who does argue reasons why someone shouldn't be a congressional representative probably exposes the flaw we look to correct through a more robust representation of peoples, beliefs, views, and experiences. Where the claim is a lack of education, we correct inadequate federal investment in the necessary education. Where the claim is that the INS test is too easy, we question whether the INS test really covers the information required for citizens to understand and perform their duties and roles. As much as we pride ourselves on being a nation of immigrants, we do also need to respect the need to preserve the values inherent in the population. "Dumping" of people into various districts, with the main intent of creating a voting bloc population reliant on government assistance, does happen, with both the populace and the immigrants frequently ending up the losers. The sooner we realize that, the better for everyone. The solution presented forces all of us to keep the focus on what is ultimately important to all free citizens in a free republic, which is knowing how to be free citizens in a free republic.

Personal Perspective

I am, by all accounts, just an ordinary citizen. I am a guy trying to earn a living and raise my family the best I know how. I am only thirty-eight years old at the time of this writing, so in many ways, I am still attempting to come up to speed on the overwhelming everything that a person needs to know to begin to make sense of all of the mind-numbingly intricate moving parts of the gigantic American machine.

I have received some of the very best public education the world has to offer. The public schools in the community where I grew up were extremely well supported. Teachers were respected members of the community. Career teachers were resented if they had become burnt out, but it was widely communicated what had gotten them there. It was a casualty of war that was well understood and honored in its own way. Far more often, older teachers were almost revered. My guidance counselor was an oracle. Teachers believed in what they did, and it was not lost on any of us.

The entire community was heavily invested in the schools and planned for their success in surprising ways. Recognizing that "poor schools" and "rich schools" were determined by factors such as parental involvement, administrators changed school boundaries to ensure that this wealth was spread evenly throughout the schools. Who knows whether this worked. Everyone hates the school boundary debate! My point is that the school district and community considered things like this because they didn't want "good schools" and "bad schools" when they could all be excellent schools!

The high school I attended offered advanced placement classes in government, history, biology, chemistry, physics, and calculus. I took them all! The government and history classes were incredible. The teachers made certain we understood the grave ramifications involved in the business of our governance at every level, in light of a full read of history. The accuracy of eyewitness accounts and the psychological tendencies of victors to always write themselves as the "good guys" were discussed to point out the judgment required in identifying truth. We delved into *The Federalist Papers, Common Sense,* the Declaration of Independence, and the Bill of Rights, exploring and discussing them in light of the events that preceded and followed them. The teacher of the advanced placement government class, James Sauer, taught the principles and arguments presented in *The Federalist Papers* to analyze the structure of various state governments and made prophetic claims regarding the difficulties we would watch those states face in our lifetime as a result of the structures they had chosen. We learned of the enormous disconnect between the values we envision and strive for as a people and the unfortunate mechanisms that must be in place in our systems of government to address our own failings in our collective abilities to attain those values.

I joined the school debate team and learned how to argue. I also quickly learned the difference between being correct and winning an argument. I was able to separate the tactical art of modern debate from the actual educational tool it used to be, and should still be, in honestly exploring competing concepts. The experience helped me to understand the vast majority of what is going on around me in the political world and on TV.

My interests and efforts paid off. I was fortunate enough to earn an appointment to the United States Air Force Academy. I joke that it was a small engineering management school that could get to know you on a *very* personal level but would still promise to treat you like a number. That was not a fair thing to say. Educationally, it was heaven. The focus on the reasons behind our government, the way it works, the way other governments work, as well as the philosophical underpinnings that form the basis of our reasoning and understanding regarding the very concepts of life, liberty, human dignity, justice, and utility were of the utmost importance.

The Air Force Academy was training people who promised to "protect the Constitution of the United States against all enemies, foreign and domestic." It was of vital importance that those individuals demonstrate a full understanding of those principals before being handed the keys to the world's largest nuclear arsenal! The lesson was clear: We must prepare people to do very real, serious business in order for them to actually be capable of doing the very real, serious business that needs to be done. The consequences for putting the nation in jeopardy by violating trust in performing these essential duties was communicated clearly and understood fully. We have an honor code, and we enforce it! It was widely recognized that skills could be taught and bad habits could be erased, with the proper focus. Good habits could be formed with adequate training. The practice of discipline was fostered, supported, and encouraged. The thinking goes that in this type of training environment, eventually people learn how to teach themselves and are then capable of dominating any environment they are put in, given the proper resources and barring superior competition.

If a violation occurred in any category of performance, giving the individual several chances to correct the issue was seen as part of the learning process. There was, however, one thing that was universally recognized as being an unacceptable character defect that could not be tolerated: dishonesty. Lying, stealing, cheating, or even tolerating it among our peers was unacceptable, and the general thinking was, "If you ain't got it by now, you prob'ly ain't never gonna get it, and we can't teach that to you!" Except for extremely rare circumstances, people who were dishonest were gone. It was that simple. They had no place in leadership.

It is also interesting to note, for those wondering where integrity was expected to be taught, that of all of the things this service academy felt it could impart on a young and impressionable human being in a reasonable amount of time, integrity was not one of them. I can't speak to the leadership training experience, or what concept of integrity is adhered to at Ivy League institutions and renowned business schools, but that's how it worked at the public schooling I received.

I ended up facing fairly serious personal difficulties in life, and a military career suddenly wasn't an option. Eventually, life led me to graduate school for clinical social work. The institution I attended helped me to learn the skills I needed to provide social services to the communities where I lived in rural Idaho. The school itself was a Seventh Day Adventist institution well respected for its program. The teachers there were all incredibly devoted individuals who were deeply committed to practicing the act of loving others through service. They explained the importance of meeting people where they are, treating them with the respect we would expect if we were in their situation, and asking them if we are unclear about how they wish to be shown respect. We should ask what our neighbor's struggles are. They explained the importance of understanding that when individuals within a community struggle, it often has a lasting impact on the community for generations to come, with the manifestation of the problem often increasing by a generational growth factor of six to eight. They explained the importance of providing, or often only suggesting, meaningful solutions to people at the right time can prevent catastrophic consequences for the individual and the community and instead pave the way for generations of joy and abundance. We studied the history of welfare laws and programs as society matured, along with human understanding and capability. I came to fully appreciate the indelible impact that the patterns of our modern society were having in the details of the lives of the individuals in the small communities where I lived.

After a number of rewarding years in private practice in rural Idaho, I transitioned back into full-time software engineering. I attained a bachelor's in computer science while at the academy, and I had worked for a couple of years as a programmer before going into social work. I specify full-time because once you get used to writing software to solve problems, you never stop, and businesses of any kind involving people are full of problems to be solved. I thoroughly enjoy the work of software engineering. It is mentally stimulating, and for a problem solver, it provides a feedback loop of satisfaction that one doesn't get when one attempts to solve people problems. The problems are clean and logical. Solutions typically work, or they do not. Efficiencies can be measured. During this time, I was blessed to get to work on some neat projects with amazingly talented people. I gained a firsthand appreciation of what the talent pool of this nation is capable of when we simply want to accomplish something! By witnessing the clear division of priorities in the American psyche, accompanied by the resulting division of outcomes for America's people, I became frustrated at a reality that was in complete discord with the core values regarding who we are as a people and, subsequently, how we govern ourselves. National crisis after crisis produced no sign of any meaningful, durable change to the fundamental systems and institutions found inadequate or, worse, culpable in any given disaster.

Eventually, I came to the conclusion that we could do better picking these "honorable people" at random. After thinking about that concept, its functional mechanics, and the features that it would intrinsically impart to a legislating body if it could actually be realized, I began to consider how it could be applied to our current constitution to produce a positive change. I reviewed the history of our constitution and its amendments in their historical context, and I reviewed *The Federalist Papers* for wisdom on the features of popular selection in the various branches of the legislature. This research led me to a solution that I believe is not only a good corrective measure for the current problems facing our nation, but also a transformative opportunity that will enable our society as a whole to rise to meet difficult challenges and take advantage of the amazing opportunities the future has in store.

In fact, my solution represents a contract with ourselves and a renewed understanding of who we are to one another, what we stand for, and what we owe to one another that reaches more closely in functional mechanism to the practically impossible ideal of having a full representation of all individual points of view.

My Preliminary Action

In exploring this idea of a full representation, I reached out to a number of people and institutions and shared my thoughts. A few folks did confess that they thought they were going to be listening to another whack job— until they heard what I had to say.

My solution ended up satisfying a number of factors I thought were important, helping me to realize how practical and possible this idea would be to communicate, understand, debate, decide on, and implement. The simplicity of the solution and the clear path toward its realization make it easy to impart only those elements I wish to change while also eliminating erroneous side effects.

The change I am calling for is an evolutionary augmentation of the current best-known working solution. I feel it is critical for us to adopt small changes to what is by any account one of the most incredible functioning governments of all time. Let's face facts. We are dealing with rich problems here, as far as governmental issues go. When we break our current issue down to its most basic level, we are essentially stuck trying to figure out how to increase productivity and competition in the economy, while some (protecting their streams of wealth) attempt to deny the ability to compete. Our current crisis is nothing more than the age-old problem of not sharing power, out of the historically well-placed fear of the change and the retaliation that usually occur. As we live longer together as a people, with more generations experiencing the benefits of a relatively rich and stable society, and with the oscillations of power ideally being less extreme in their volume, duration, and impact, we hope we will be able to break the behavioral cycles that continue to keep us from recognizing the obligation we have to one another as neighbors, countrymen, and, at the very least, the distant cousins we actually are.

We have a system that is actively increasing its capabilities of authoritative control over the people. This system lacks fail-safes to reliable representation within the timeline needed to ensure that damages from abuses are not critical and irreparable to the offended parties. What I mean by that is if 99 percent of us can be effectively marginalized with the technologies of yesterday, what chance would any single subset of the American population have tomorrow? This is not Orwellian; entire classes of people who have been denied adequate inclusion in the legislative process throughout our short history stand as witnesses. Technology and gentrification have allowed legislators to grow distant from the common needs of those they represent. This danger was a vital consideration at the time the constitution was drafted. It is also mentioned throughout *The Federalist Papers*. It is a fact, and it needs to be addressed. Our ancestors found themselves in a similar situation when debating the formation of the republic, and this same danger informed the other considerations they took into account.

- The need for a stable form of government that would unite the confederate states, or in our case, the various factions of power, money, and the rest of us

- The need to provide national and individual security

- The need for safeguards against sedition

- The need for safeguards against faction

- The need for safeguards against tyranny and corruption that permeate the system past a point of return within the bounds of the same system

This last one is called "catastrophic failure." The good news is that we aren't close to that.

Ideally, the system should be flexible enough that it allows for disparate societies to slowly form a national identity and resolve stark regional differences in cultural norms and societal expectations, in continuation of the vision and tradition established by our founding fathers during the First Continental Congress.

In late 2013, after initially identifying the key issues and formalizing the basis of a solution in my mind, I e-mailed the Idaho secretary of state and the Idaho attorney general's office, requesting clarification on the regulations for a third political party to be formally recognized within the state (see my copy of the e-mail on pages 24–26). I did this because I concluded that both existing political parties were so entrapped in their own dysfunction that I doubted any change could be initiated through either of them. I am still firm in those convictions, and since I sent that e-mail, both parties have provided ample evidence to confirm their questionable value and lack of coherent integrity.

However, since my initial exploration of recognizing a third party, I have come to believe that this would not necessarily make things better. It could actually make things worse, if not done correctly. We already have two world-class examples of wrong to deal with at the moment. If everyone comes to understand the issue as I do and believes in the solution I have proposed, using the existing respective party members to take control of their respective party leadership structures is ideal. My concerns are systemic and nonpartisan. Partisan issues will still need to be addressed and debated, and once a system is created that can offer that environment, the two healthy parties will need to get busy actually having meaningful debates and establishing working, accountable legislation! In addition, the single issue of whether a government shall be accountable to its populace is a matter that is settled business in the American debate. The numbers demand not a third party, but a complete shift away from the parties themselves. We need to recognize that historically, leadership *within both parties* has endorsed and repeatedly attempted to enshrine within our public consciousness a segregated multiclass society as "the new old normal," with varying success. All of this comes at a time when technological innovation stands poised to unlock value and capability to humanity in general that promises the potential to usher in a new era of greater individual freedom. At the very least, it will continue to change the patterns of how we go about our lives. In fact, our generation has seen this taking place unlike any other generation in recorded history, and that trend is not slowing down.

I believe we have a solution to the core issues preventing the majority of the populace from being the constant and unavoidable anchoring voice of sanity and moral reasoning within the legislature. We have a solution that will allow we who are equal owners in the American enterprise to claim the rights of our collective citizenship in the form of the unalienable responsibility we have to ourselves through our government in ensuring all aspects of the government are accountable to all in those matters that affect us all.

I have thought more about the steps we must all take together to bring about the subtle changes I feel are necessary in order to tilt a system that is, in aggregate effect, a usurper and a predator to one that operates as the companion to all of American society that it was intended to be. Throughout the last few years, while refining the ideas and concepts I formed and discovered during my research, conversations, and reflections, I have become extremely hopeful for our future. I get the sense that in America and much of the rest of the world, we are on the precipice of what could be an age of unprecedented growth, peace, and prosperity, both in the material and existential sense, if we could simply harness and cultivate the amazing strength of character and abilities that are abundantly evident in our citizens! My hope and prayer is that simply though talking, debating, and making a collective decision to take action, the rest of the world will watch us peacefully and amicably choose a different way to govern that more accurately reflects the free and great people of our nation and our unfailing commitment to liberty and justice for all, and they will see us use it to make liberty and justice for all a reality among ourselves!

> From: Matthew Wells Sanders
> Sent: Tuesday, August 20, 2013 11:04 PM
> To: SOSinfoDL
> Subject: Reform Party: Seeking Information regarding petition format
>
> Mr. Secretary,
>
> I am extremely serious about the following request. I am the chair for the Reform Party in Idaho. Having read through 34-501, I would like a copy of a valid petition as described in part (1), section (c), subsection (E):
>
> "(E) The format of the signature petition sheets shall be prescribed by the secretary of state and shall be patterned after, but not limited to, such sheets as used for state initiative and referendum measures."
>
> ACTION ITEM: Please forward me a copy of this petition.
>
> Reading through the statutes, I am of the understanding that after August 30 of this year, I will be able to begin gathering "signatures of at least a number of qualified electors equal to two per cent (2%) of the aggregate vote cast for presidential electors in the state at the previous general election at which presidential electors were chosen."
>
> ACTION ITEM: What would that (2%) entail in terms of head count, or what was the aggregate vote cast for presidential electors in the state at the previous general election at which presidential electors were chosen so that I can calculate the percentage?

I am very serious about perusing the establishment of the "Reform Party" as a recognized party in the state of Idaho, as well as throughout the nation. My main goal is to bring systemic change to how one of the houses of our national bicameral legislature are selected to more meaningfully represent the people, while providing more thorough and accountable oversight of those institutions which currently have no meaningful oversight.

I find it deeply troubling that the government has taken it upon itself to hold the populace completely accountable, while subverting the Constitution of the United States. It is time for accountability to be the cause of the people with regards to its government with the goal of preserving a government "by the people, for the people."

Additionally, I find it troubling that our Republic now represents mere dollars as opposed to popular vote in any form of its branches.

A historical look at the structure of the two houses will show that both were not always selected by "popular vote." At this point in time, I believe that the Federal system is broken and in need of systemic refactoring to avoid what appears to be an unsustainable course.

With that in mind, I am seeking this information to begin recruiting like-minded individuals to stand with us in reforming a broken system.

We, as a nation, are facing issues that are unprecedented in our nation's history, and without at least one half of a functioning legislative body that is immune to campaign finance, both public, private, domestic, foreign, personal, and corporate, we, as a people will not be able to effectively hold the debates necessary to be self-deterministic as a populace. Instead, decisions would continue to be made for us by an "incestuous" few who use money as an abstraction of political power to undermine policies that would strengthen our nation, and instead would enrich themselves creating further wealth disparity.

Since recent polls show Congress has a lower approval rating than some venereal diseases, that money can quantitatively be shown to change election outcomes, that many corporations are staffed by individuals "owned" by the same "entities" that "purchase" their interests from current law-makers, and that law-makers themselves are now considering non-transparency in the legislative process (even on tax code issues), I believe that picking individuals from a Voluntary selective service pool (if of proper age as defined in the U.S. Constitution, and can pass the INS test that we use to naturalize citizens) would compose a legislative body that would be immune to corporate issues unlike anything we have had in the recent past. Every two years, the populace could opt to vote that member out to be replaced, at random in lottery-ball style. This method has been used to select young men who readily fought and died to defend the Constitution of the United States against all enemies, both foreign and domestic. Instead, we have a system that is currently violating both the spirit and intent of many of the basic amendments of the aforementioned founding document.

I believe strongly that we stand at a tipping point, and I propose a peaceful solution to this systemic political/economic dysfunction. I realize that this sort of movement will take time, and patience, but will only grow more appealing as an obvious solution as wealth disparity grows and the vast majority of the populace becomes even more disenfranchised.

I appreciate your time and consideration in reading this request, and await the form listed in the statute.

ACTION ITEM: For clarification, would THIS August 30th (an odd numbered year) be a year preceding a general election year in 2014?

Again, thank you for your time, and I look forward to a digital copy of this form within the next 10 business days.

I will also pass a copy of this message to the Attorney General in case any other clarification is necessary.

Respectfully,

Matthew Wells Sanders

We live in what can still be regarded the most interesting, and historically unprecedented experiments in human freedom in all of recorded history. The pace of technological improvements, the rate at which we can exchange information, and our collective manufacturing capability have changed society in fundamental ways. However, not all changes have proportionately benefited the population. In the United States and across much of the developed world, wealth distribution is such that a relatively small fraction of the population holds the vast majority of the wealth. This situation has been steadily getting worse since the 1970s and shows no sign of reversing itself. To make matters worse, candidates for public office are increasingly reliant on considerable sources of funding to run for election. This pay-for-play political system ensures that the monetary wealth of the extreme few has an outsized voice in shaping policy. The policies being affected by this extreme wealth—such as the tax code, social policies that empower labor, trade laws that can exploit labor in both countries simultaneously, and a patent system that is used to stifle innovation and competition—almost invariably serve to enrich the same small percentage of individuals. This feedback loop is strengthened by political tactics such as gerrymandering, removing voting locations from the immediate access of communities, or creating other inhibitors that prevent specific populations from sharing their political voice. Even now, in the 2016 presidential election, we have a "Democratic" National Committee that has been exposed as corrupt in its primary process for its presidential candidate, undermining the very process that defines us as a free and self-deterministic society.

On the other side of the aisle, voters who have free reign have presented a candidate that is as unpalatable to the party leadership as the party leadership is to its party people. To exacerbate the situation, our political and financial systems and the laws pertaining to their regulation are extremely complex. Attempts to enact legislation to try to correct issues that seem to be the source of complete dysfunction seem to fail poorly. The compromise that takes place to even get the legislation passed renders such legislation completely ineffective. If the laws are passed, they can be ignored through lack of enforcement, either by administrative policy or by a defunding of the entities providing enforcement and oversight.

The Supreme Court recently decided that it would not uphold prosecution for outright bribery of an elected official, admitting it would be too difficult to identify proper corruption from the prevailing understanding of "business as usual." This is after the same court ruled that an unlimited amount of money should be allowed into the political process. In other words, the government that found the financial system as too big to fail has also found the corruption flowing back into the political system as too big to fail as well, under the argument that it is too big to regulate.

In summary, the United States does not have a form of government that represents the populace when it comes to choosing legislative representatives. We have a government that is representative of dollar bills, and all three branches openly acknowledge this. This is a structural problem that we *must* address immediately and that will require a similar change to the constitution as has been done in the past on the same issues of a corrupt legislative branch. If the current situation continues unchanged, the credibility of the basis of our entire political and economic system will fall into legitimate question.

TIME FOR ACTION

We are standing at a tipping point, and I propose a peaceful solution to this systemic political-economic dysfunction. This sort of movement will take time and patience but will only grow more appealing as an obvious solution as wealth disparity grows, as the vast majority of the populace becomes even more disenfranchised, and as the hard math of the economic problem as we have forced ourselves to define it becomes clearly unsolvable to everyone.

In short, I mean to establish the inalienable right of every capable citizen to be a direct participant in the legislative process in a manner that can no longer be ignored, marginalized, or forgotten with time, and that defines our controlling stake as owners. The following amendment (see pages 29–30), in conjunction with the societal changes it demands, will strengthen and enrich our nation in ways that cannot be valued in terms of mere money. The capacity for material excess will be increased as a natural byproduct of the human potential that will be unlocked immediately and through the generational reshaping of the population's mindset, policies, behaviors, and relationships with one another and their respective communities.

The solution I lay out before you in this amendment, the tactical approach towards implementation and ratification, and the further thoughts for consideration are the result of one person's concern that something is fundamentally wrong and is threatening the peace and stability of our society—yet no one is doing anything about it. It is the result of years of focused thought, reflection, self-doubt, and careful consideration. I present this solution at the time others appear to be more than ready and willing to act but, until now, have lacked a unified purpose and plan.

I ask only what others before me have asked in our history as a nation. Read what I have to say. Weigh it for the value of the ideas expressed and their relevance to reality as you can confirm it for yourself. Where you find fault and disagree, please consider what remains of value, and if the remainder still promises undeniable relief from at least a subset of confirmed societal ills, join me and take the House!

Proposed Constitutional Amendment

The "Take the House" Amendment

The House of Representatives shall be composed of members chosen by random lottery of all eligible citizens who have volunteered for the selection pool.

Every second year, the people of the states will vote to retain or dismiss their representatives on an individual basis. Upon a vote of dismissal or a vacancy, a new lottery will be immediately held.

No person shall be a representative who has not attained to the age of twenty-five years, has not been seven years a citizen of the United States, has not passed the naturalization civics test as required of naturalized citizens by law, or will not, when elected, be an inhabitant of that congressional district in which he or she shall be chosen.

At the time of this writing, if adopted and ratified, this would become the twenty-eight amendment to the constitution. It would update Article 1, section 2. I believe that this amendment would immediately produce some very real and lasting effects, and it would allow and encourage other beneficial changes to progress over time.

Objectives

1. **Grant the rights of ownership in the American enterprise to every citizen through access to direct participation in systems of the legislature, including executing its duties and functions.**

All of us have a claim to ownership in this nation's governance. That liberty, which we all hold dear, is only as real as the laws we create pertaining to it and our ability to both adhere to and enforce those laws. The common pattern in our nation's history regarding the obvious difference between our recognized beliefs on human rights and equality under the law and our beliefs in practice tells the tale of a reliable increase in an understanding of ourselves and of the resulting evolution of government to reflect that increased understanding, ever in line with our stated beliefs. Enshrining that sense of ownership for every class of member in society in a means that cannot discriminate and that gives access to the duties and powers of the legislature itself is a strong leap toward ensuring a government "of the people, by the people, and for the people" (Lincoln, "The Gettysburg Address"). Any number of civil rights issues, both well-known and yet unrealized, will be far more easily addressed and even directly represented within the legislature.

2. **Confer the natural responsibilities of ownership in the American enterprise to every citizen through requirements of direct participation in systems of legislature.**

Similar to the former objective, this one points to the minimal requirement of passing a test that shows a basic understanding of the function and role of our government and our rights and laws as outlined in the constitution itself. I have included this requirement for a few reasons. I wanted to seed some conversation in the public arena that should inform obvious considerations on related topics. We need to take a thorough and honest appraisal of what is educationally required of a citizen to properly prepare him or her for participating in the legislative process, in addition to his or her being educated enough to know what information to request and what values to consider in making wise decisions in the matters on which he or she is asked to make decisions. We have clearly determined that there is a minimum acceptable level of knowledge for an immigrant to become a citizen. The rest of us need the benefit of this constant reminder as well. Near the end of this short book, I cover some very specific suggestions on educational considerations that are necessary to maintaining a healthy society, but like most problems that are pervasive, they are best left to a legislature of more fit representation and authority on handling such matters.

3. **Remove money from the campaign process and reduce monetary influence and reliance in the decision-making process.**

At least one-half of the bicameral legislature would have money removed from the campaign process. Although money would still be spent campaigning against specific individuals, the replacement would be picked at random. This prevents a stacking of the deck.

Under the proposed system, we would pay Congress enough to be public servants who are monitored heavily for conflicts of interest. They would accept no funds from any outside sources and would have no campaign to benefit from contributions. Their tenure would be based purely on the satisfaction of the constituency. Limits on negative advertising specific to a single candidate would be naturally limited in direct proportion to the amount of equal response that is deemed economically appropriate for a representative to attempt to clarify his or her positions to the constituency. This would help arrest the "arms race" scenario of game theory that has fueled the economic spending of campaigns to such morally dubious but predictable heights. Specifically, it addresses the matter by avoiding a court that has exposed some interesting constraints on the matter by equating campaign spending to speech.

Greed in Politics

For the last few decades, our system of government has actively worked to protect the wealth and status of an extreme minority of the population. The wealthy have effectively applied corporate strategies to capture the board of the American enterprise by ensuring legislators, judges, and members of the executive branch reinforce a system that now seems to respond to only the single stimulus of cash. The middle class, once a strong political voice for the populace, has been decimated. If workers demanded basic human rights or more reasonable compensation, their jobs were sent overseas to workers who could not secure such rights. The lesson the rich Americans hoped the laborers would learn was "Don't be greedy." The lesson American laborers actually learned was that the government would not protect the American way of life over profits for a few and would allow businesses on an international level to leverage the same predatory practices that had been used earlier in our nation's history to pit individual states against one another, maximizing human exploitation on both sides of the border.

Laws that were put in place due to hard lessons learned by our grandparents regarding the natural inclination of finance and banking to be corrupt and to destroy the lending mechanisms that made necessities of human existence (such as home and land ownership) possible were removed, with predictable results. As the tax base erodes, local city and state programs that the public relies on disappear, and public utilities fall into disrepair. As corporations abandon these towns and states, the towns and states are left with all of the debt, both financial and social.

When promises are broken, the majority of people always come out the loser. A predictable tiny fraction of people always come out the winner, while telling the losers through the news outlets they own that "the government doesn't pick winners." Common-sense solutions or calls for basic accountability go nowhere; they seem to violate some unspoken rule that would "destroy life as we know it."

The entity of money itself has been given the title of speech by the courts, so that no one dare impede its communication. However, the message seems to be clear to the recipients only. The rest of us are not privy to the conversation. Corporations are given the status of people, without the benefit of any individual accountability. In a nation that has a precedent of having to break up technological monopolies due to the known limits of economic theory, we carry on today with false duopolies. Some companies are set up solely for the purpose of having the appearance of competition in an industry. The system is rigged and corrupt. It does not even pretend to be otherwise at this point.

Under the surface, there is an attitude that resents the "stupid American people," and that believes the weak and stupid among us should be allowed to die off. Paying taxes is universally regarded as something that serves only the "undeserving, lazy, uneducated poor." Taxes are not paid by the companies that owe their existence to American education, labor, infrastructure, culture, and historical investment of blood, sweat, and tears. The populations that support and produce talented individuals watch those individuals enter a workforce that will never give back to the local community. The public and private companies they work for do not feel any obligation to America's rural communities as a whole. Corporations are defined first by their legal obligation to maximize profits before all other concerns, and their concerns have been placed well ahead of the populace at large. The promise has always been that wealth would flow down from the top, but we have experienced the opposite. The numbers do not lie. When everyone is put on mute and all we are left with is the reality of our collective behaviors, the evidence is depressing and damning.

Over the course of our short history, the situation with our form of government has always looked the same. Metaphorically speaking, people at the front of the caravan fight for control every few years to figure out who is going to determine the course for the caravan. Some people are moved closer to the front, and others are moved to the back. Some are left in the desert, and others are killed. Some are thrown into the wagons of others.

As technology has progressed and the immediate consequences that an entire people face have increased to almost philosophically comical proportions, so has the metaphor. To the American people, it now appears that we are all on a large space shuttle as opposed to a wandering caravan. The danger, consequences, and uncertainty seem far more immediate and severe to the whole. Cameras and intercoms are able to broadcast the fight for the cockpit to the entire shuttle and to those watching from other countries. In addition to the increased tension in the changeovers at the cockpit over the last few decades, there is a strong sense that some of us are in the booster rocket, and others are afraid of being thrown out of the shuttle altogether. There is also a sense that the rocket has been hijacked to provide a joyride for a few to an undisclosed location—or worse, no one is really attempting to fly this thing, and the flight crew members are the only ones wearing parachutes! If I had to guess, the American people would have no problem enforcing very appropriate rules for what goes on near the cockpit of our enterprise.

If you are like me, you are furious. You realize that a small group of very wealthy and powerful people are attempting to establish themselves as modern royalty, viewing our republic as simply another parent organization that needs to be usurped and controlled. These few have tricked us into allowing them grotesque profit margins and payouts and picking winners, all the while claiming a level playing field. Lady Justice wears a pirate's eye patch. As larger portions of the American population are pushed toward poverty, policies with the effect of keeping us divided abound and appear to be coordinated across the globe. We see it as other extremist groups attempting to attack us here at home. In retaliation, we go to war against "them." As the communities that support the populace deteriorate in these faraway places, and as poverty breeds outrage in the people over real oppression, lack of opportunity, and a strong sense that those in power are keeping them in their current state with the aid of the United States and her allies, our communities experience a similar poverty. We participate in these wars to "defeat the enemy" and sometimes remove a "leader," only to find we have no reasonable suggestions to a newly freed people on how to proceed, grow, and develop as a society. In those countries, we quickly witness well-defined religious groups grabbing power from others, and those who finally lose access to the political system also lose any and all security.

We like to hold ourselves up in our own minds as a people and nation that represent and embody great causes of freedom, opportunity, justice, and equality. Instead, we appear to be hypocrites unto ourselves, because our biggest thieves remain in their jobs and continue to openly bribe our politicians. Our own system of government does not provide any type of mechanism to effectively protect against factions seizing and consolidating exclusive power to the detriment of entire classes of humanity. We end up becoming a curse to all regular families in a foreign country when, from their perspective, we do "liberate" them; we offer them the fire as opposed to the frying pan. Then, taking the only other reasonable recourse, they flee to their neighbors to find those people and their governments resentful of them as individuals!

We can and must do better than that. We have far more to offer ourselves and the world.

The Ethics Problem

After the most recent financial collapse in our country, Alan Greenspan and others expressed shock and amazement that bankers would collectively derail the economy. I don't get the impression that Greenspan was crying alligator tears. Rather, I get the impression he really thought those making decisions at the heads of financial institutions would be smart enough to not blow up their own market. This admits an outlook that trusted the people within the banking and finance industry to be self-regulating, ignoring the basic principles of the tragedy of the commons. In hindsight, it confirms that trust cannot be given to those individuals and that the entire system is a complete joke in terms of regulation and enforcement in practice, due to the obvious thought of the leadership that has defined the entire environment over the last couple of generations. Because there has been no change whatsoever in the attitudes of anyone who either designed the derailment in the first place or allowed it to happen, much less any firing of the leadership/management/board within the finance industries or the government, we can safely predict the same results from the same institutions in the future. One only has to look to our nation's nuclear chain of command to see what is done to leadership in response to underlings cheating on a paper test to figure out what should happen to the entire lot of them if we agree that their industry is vital to safeguarding American interests. We didn't get that kind of response, obviously.

Even worse, lawsuits against a major banking institution a decade later make the obviously reasonable claim that, even recently, the culture within these institutions actively sought out and got rid of individuals attempting to adhere to the law—not to say anything about ethics during the performance of their jobs—with some notable results. This simply ensured that this institution was filled with unethical people at every level, and logically many others like it, as I am sure this is an accurate microcosm of a majority of industries and areas of government across America where it is common knowledge that "Good people just won't cut it here." They effectively solved their whistle-blower problem by artificially creating a situation wherein only the unethical could remain, tainting the remaining workforce by rewarding unethical and illegal behavior as the law of the land. I would imagine that this is a sentiment familiar to a lot of you, no matter what you do, because systemic attitudes end up becoming societal norms. This also assured that ethical people would be out of a job (and probably out of an industry), take a real hit in their pay, probably lose some property, and definitely not have time and energy to apply their ethical idiosyncrasy to anything where they might do damage to another business that is too big to fail. This taught the lesson that not only are unethical and illegal behaviors rewarded, but adherence to ethical values, or even adherence to the expectation of rule of law, is a real threat to their personal property, security, and livelihood. Therefore good people do finish last— by careful design.

I propose that the same attitudes and practices guiding our business ethics are prevalent in our political system as well. By ensuring a body of representatives who are not in debt to someone by their very nature, the Take the House Amendment will protect our legislators from a toxic environment that prevents ethical people from being able to legislate from their beliefs and values as citizens experiencing the reality of American society firsthand. I believe it will give America its sense of soul, which seems to be missing today.

Money as Power

While studying at the Air Force Academy, I took some electrical engineering classes. One of the classes covered the theory and operation of the three-phase electric grid. A principle that intrigued me at the time, and that I still think about to this day, is that of active and reactive power and the loss of total observable, or apparent, power flowing through a set of lines when an inductive load is placed on the system. In plain speak, it goes something like this.

The power company registers a new customer. This customer runs a great deal of electric motors, like a saw mill or a trash-processing facility. These electric motors cause a special type of resistance, called impedance, that shifts the voltage and current wave forms so that they are not in phase, or in sync, with one another, resulting in an inability for most utilities to accurately account for the power consumed. Because the grid is truly too big to fail, and the system must be balanced all the time, the power company must develop a solution to maintain the overall mathematical sanity of the system. The answer is a capacitor bank, or some other similar electro-mechanical device that can correct the phase shift and keep the power use of the customer in a form that is both safe and accountable to the federated power grid. For the opposite problem, a similar compensating solution exists.

The American political system is in a situation SO similar in its logical symptoms that it begs the question as to why comparable solutions have not been implemented, but for the obvious and damning reality. Money, a device of secondary creation by our government, has been granted unlimited flow into the political machinery. This affords it the status of real political power, outweighing traditional factors, such as pervading popular opinion. With wealth concentrated in the hands of so few, these few can use their monetary power and influence, either through cash donated directly to politicians and their campaigns, or through the saturation of media outlets via political propaganda. This power can effectively diminish, or render ineffective, other traditional sources of power or checks to its abuse, such as the representatives needing to stand morally accountable to the people they would return to in resuming their daily occupations after holding office. In fact, the power of money is increased exponentially by the overall statistical dominance of modern media in shaping even local opinions on issues with respect to every other traditional form of value formation.

This makes sense and is a common feature of humanity to socially gravitate toward a perceived socially accepted norm. We saw it in the prevailing beliefs of the white Baptist churches in the South during slavery, showing that no matter what you state you believe, you will in all statistical probability believe what you think you see others around you believing through their words and actions. Media is able to lie to us and spout garbage in our eyes and ears all day long. The politicians have millions of reasons to thank a few people the first day they hit office. Their constituents, uneducated and unorganized, form their opinions on the representatives' candidacy through whatever message the television and advertising producers try to tell.

In all of this, the public's ability and duty to understand what is going on in the political decision-making process is thoroughly undermined in a number of ways. They have difficulty getting access to the information they need and cannot make an informed decision regarding which possible candidates would offer proper representation. In fact, many of the inherent justifications that were present at the time of the writing of *The Federalist Papers,* which caused the authors to dismiss the idea of Congressmen being able to effectively wall themselves off from the cares of their constituency, have vanished.

Our legislature, I would argue, has become something that sees itself as a class and profession unto itself, and the amount of power we the constituents used to wield through political discourse in our communities, at our jobs, in our churches, and in the bars has vanished as well. It has been replaced by the one-way broadcast media outlets of the Internet and TV, giving the impression of a connection to a community spirit. There is an "accounting problem" with this sort of situation. Because of the obfuscation monetary power introduces when translated fairly directly to real political power, we are unable to ascertain who is using how much power, and who benefits and loses.

But it gets worse. Because the legislative process then actively picks winners and losers, determining who will profit and who will lose in any variety of situations within the economy, it creates a cycle wherein the wealth of the top 1 percent is elevated, in conjunction with the political class, to an economic advantage that erases the ability for the rest of us to claim and keep any property in durable fashion. The power industry also sees runaway feedback situations like this as well, with explosive results.

This is not a joke, and this is not a game. This is far more serious than the electric grid. Some things aren't for sale! Our systems of legislation and justice, and the execution of both, are precisely those things. It is time for a "capacitor bank" to be introduced into the solution for all of the same reasons.

Later in my professional career, I had the distinct pleasure of working for a small company that provided technological solutions to the power industry. The company tagline stood out to me: "Making electric power safer, more reliable, and more economical." As I worked there as an engineer, I was also still developing these ideas in my mind. While thinking of aspects of "real power" in the electrical realm and the various problems presented through its codification, standardization, utilization, and implementation in various societies, I pondered the wisdom of applying the same slogan to the current issue of political and monetary power in our utility of government. Incidentally, that company I worked for is employee owned. They feel it gives them a number of distinct advantages in the industry, and I am inclined to agree. In the same manner, I believe it is time for us all to claim the same employee ownership, and work to make the power of government safer, more reliable, and more economical, mutually sharing in the various forms of the rich profits of our endeavors. Needless to say, my experience in that industry was one of deep insight, rich with reward.

Random representative selection from a pool of qualified candidates will effectively erase the need for the campaign circus that helps to fuel the incestuous corruption of the legislature. We would be able to remind citizens that when they serve the public in the capacity of the Congress, they are public servants, under oath, who must be free from the appearance of wrongdoing. They should be able to place any and all business into the hands of a third-party fiduciary, and to be held to a far higher standard than the rest of the American population when it comes to the consequences of being bought off. Pretend they are a minority that took one thousand dollars from a store they worked at, or something that would make sense to you and me—and then multiply that consequence by about a thousand in your brain to reflect the magnified impact their collusion, corruption, and theft would have on the rest of us.

The benefit shouldn't be seen as purely punitive, however. We still want our members of Congress to accept payouts and bribes! Hear me out! This is their job, and this was the original intent all along. This is where some seriously effective pimps are necessary. They should be acting as the protectors of their market, always working with businesses to maximize the profitability of the returns of any enterprise to the ongoing enrichment and continuity of the populace they serve! In other words, the legislator is concerned only about the overall improvement in the quality of life of his or her constituents. The legislator *should* be looking for payouts—just not for himself or herself, but for the community as a whole.

That being said, I am sure the future Congress would have no problem negotiating a compensation package that would help to keep them honest. I have always considered that practice to be some of the best money ever spent. There is truly value in that, but it requires starting with the honest! We may need to cycle almost the whole current system out in order to do that, and a little randomization would go a long way to that end in an extremely short amount of time. One only needs to look to Nevada to see that the government already recognizes the power of randomization in creating a fair gaming market. They have extremely specific laws regarding how random number generation must be done to ensure a clever individual with a computer can't game the system and tell the future with perfect accuracy. We need this feature! This is the mechanism by which we are being robbed of far more than property. For better or for worse, we are all required to play at this casino, and it currently impacts everything we hold dear.

To sum all this up, we can strip money out of politics. It's quite simple if we are at all serious about it, as is shown by the proposed Take the House Amendment. Part of the elegant simplicity of this solution is how well it does exactly that. We have some priorities completely upside down within the culture of our political institutions, and they need to be addressed fully and thoroughly over the next few decades, starting now! We need money to step aside for a bit so we can get a full accounting of the flow of power as a first step toward the beginnings of accountability within our government.

Money as Speech

The Supreme Court has used the findings of a case from 1976 in which it was determined that limiting campaign contributions in any way was a violation of the first amendment. A majority of justices at the time said money is an expression of speech, and in doing so, they felt there should be no law restricting campaign contributions. Not all the judges felt this way, and the clear risks that unlimited contributions would entail were noted at the time. Since the seventies, several laws have been put into place to control the effects of unlimited campaign finance, but most of them have been removed or weakened to the point of irrelevance by the repeated assertion that money is speech.

As a result, today we have unlimited cash in the campaign process. This means we have a legalized graft system whereby challengers must gain corporate sponsorship, like a race car, in order to compete. Conversely, popular candidates openly accept "tribute" from anyone expecting their issues to be considered and supported. Enormous amounts of money are spent on digital advertising to market the "competing products" to the viewing American public. Industries compete to own entire bloc of politicians to make sure their interests are protected. This makes politicians rich, and it keeps the rich rich. Essentially, the judiciary argued against restricting the flow of money into the various holes of the political machinery by equating money itself to speech in modern society. This is actually a good argument when you apply it one way, but it leaves out some crucial aspects of the nature of money and the reality of a bribe when applied in this context.

The Problem with Money's Unrestrained Influence in Politics

1. *It effectively removes concepts of morality and right and wrong from any decision-making process. It opens the door to readily making decisions that grotesquely violate human rights in word and deed.*

   The more money allowed into the campaign process, the more money necessary to win office. The more you owe to your victory, the more you owe *for* your victory. If every representative and politician owes his or her job, in a very real sense, to money first and to whomever paid it to them second, the whole thing's corrupt! It can't be otherwise! Although the mechanisms of the system appear to be functioning correctly, it is tainted to the core.

2. *It creates the scenario wherein politicians are trained to seek the appropriate answers to popular needs from corporations and extremely wealthy individuals first (and often only).*

   The secondary part of the power transfer occurs in the "picking winners" and "protecting vital interests" activities in which this purchased government engages. I am claiming quite boldly that this is the basis of a class-action-type mass fraud on the American public. There will never be any legal claim or remedy for the actions of the past, because the scope of it would include concepts of monopoly, bribery, price fixing, and other activities usually associated with organized crime and gambling, which fail to be identified and regulated. One can never claim a crime for a law that conveniently didn't exist at the time. The lack of accountability that is fostered to create a path to pay our public servants is returned back to the investor. In all of the statistics we look at from the last few decades, that one fact remains clear.

3. *The influence of money reverses the intended loyalty of the representative.*

This reversal of loyalty is what allows the representative's fellow citizens to be taken advantage of and treats them as markets to be exploited rather than markets to be protected. This is the exact opposite of what is required of legislators in this land!

Frankly, the arguments that have come out of the Supreme Court on topics of money and political power do little to paint the judiciary as a champion of justice. They identify values worth defending but do so in a grossly dishonest way. It is as if they mean to set up an unsolvable legal problem for us to perpetuate legalized bribery!

My Thoughts on the Idea of Money as Speech

The court misused a logical argument to allow the purchase of our political system by the wealthy. We cannot trust the courts to make a wise decision for the American people, and the courts have shown that they will eliminate all efforts to control bribery of our politicians. We must have a solution that cannot be destroyed by a judiciary that is complicit in the bribery, and I think this amendment does that very well. This is an admittedly frustrating situation to be in, because there are aspects of the metaphorical comparison that hold very true, while the dangers and need for limiting that specific form of expression are as obvious as the consequences for making fake bomb threats in a crowded movie theater. Finding the appropriate balance is required and requires extremely good judgment. It is apparent to me, at this point in time, that our current judicial system is in no position to provide the reliable judgment needed to protect the republic or the American populace on these matters. They have sold out as well.

By eliminating the campaign system for the members of the house, you effectively lower the cost of lobbying issues dramatically. You actually render free actually spoken speech more free, effective, and efficient when seen from the perspective of the message. If we are going to play in the land of monetary metaphor as previous Supreme Court justices have done, this remark deserves supreme consideration. I have graciously accepted the logical argument presented by the earlier court and offer a solution that does not rely on their supplying any moral leadership or judgment whatsoever and that removes the issue that threatens the integrity of the government itself, doing the double damage of insulting the logical constructs of both money and speech while doing so. The members of the House of Representatives can now be monitored like jury members or, say, members of a special elite government unit managing the nation's most critical business for financial or other conflicts of interest. I can safely assume the courts understand how to do that effectively, and where the unlimited speech of money might be problematic in an environment where public trust is paramount in deriving any authority for the institution itself!

It is unfortunate that history has faithfully shown us that the Supreme Court can mostly be relied upon to find it "just and right" to preserve the right for portions of the populace to exploit other portions, and it is even more unfortunate to see that reality still present in today's judicial leaders. So be it. If the statement of the courts is effectively, "If you don't like it, vote them out, and if you can't, you don't deserve to try to run the country," then I see no other option than to take their advice to the letter, avoiding any approach that might involve their future opinion on the matter.

My solution takes this into full consideration, handling the core of the corruption issue in the constitutional change itself, which should place it soundly outside of the jurisdiction of the courts on any level. Any secondary change to bring a system of internal accountability, such as an honor code, to the legislators themselves is also a change that invites no check or balance from the executive or judicial branches. If we the people end up finding the judicial and executive branches need rebalancing in terms of their current power and authority, we will have at least one branch we can more fully trust from which to wield reliable power to that end.

4. Increase representation of the needs of the populace in the debate and formation of the national legislation.

Money currently rules advertisement and marketing, which drives the campaign process, with rare exception. The primary process has increasingly ensured that the candidates who are elected are divided so severely along fringe ideology that the greater needs of the electorate are lost. The media and monetary interests have successfully exploited this to create a system wherein the greater needs of the overall electorate can be almost completely ignored in the political process. Obviously, all of that changes greatly if the House of Representatives doesn't owe anything to anyone but their constituencies when doing their jobs.

5. Reduce the need to gerrymander districts.

Gerrymandering is another tool used to stack the decks to maintain political control by the parties without regard to representing the will or needs of the electorate. Under this new system, gerrymandering becomes far less beneficial and prevalent. The degree to which an interest would continue to invest considerable time and resources to securing a district will be weighed against the reality that, once lost, their investment has no bearing on the probable loyalties of the replacement. Removing the effectiveness and incentive for these types of behaviors will effectively address all manner of ills, some of which we may not even be aware of!

6. Decrease the ability for special interests to rig the political system in a targeted fashion.

Through the use of campaign contributions, gerrymandering, and cherry-picking key races, heavily monetized interests have been able further their agenda to a level that is unsafe to the future of the republic.

This trend needs to be arrested. The amount of concentrated wealth and sophisticated polling, marketing, surveillance, and computing available make this a very real and present danger to the health of our nation and economy. The only realistic way to counterbalance this unforeseen game change in popular behavior is to introduce a healthy amount of entropy into the system while preserving the right of the electorate to remove a representative, yet still ensuring that all classes of citizens have a durable, irrevocable mechanism by which their presence and opinion cannot be ignored. Where we need to review what protections are necessary to shield the selection pool of candidates and the serving representatives from domestic and foreign exploitation, we naturally review what is required to protect us all.

I am blatantly saying that smart groups of people and, soon, computers that can already make our smartest look like fools at the chessboard and on the stock market are constantly trying to figure out how to manipulate the system to gain power and money, often undermining and destroying the institutions themselves to get their way. I point out that we have already lost that battle, as evidenced by our current state of affairs, and I believe randomization in the selection process provides a startling amount of defense against even the highly capable theoretical political threats at the bounds of our capabilities. I would point out that we actually do have to worry about James Bond supervillain types of scenarios. This isn't a game.

7. Maintain the Senate as a voice of monetized special interest.

The bicameral legislature was historically selected with differing approaches. The Senate, prior to the passage of the seventeenth amendment, was selected through the states' legislatures. This approach restores the differing means of selecting the halves of the bicameral legislature in much of the same spirit of the founding fathers. Members of Congress selected from a more diverse cross-section of American life without ties to the large pool of monetary control (which is in fewer hands than ever before) will arguably have far more allegiance to their states and will presumably argue correctly where the delineation between states' rights and federal mandate lies.

Understanding that the majority faction must be kept in check, the Senate will act as that buffer. However, because they are fewer, and their districts represent a larger percentage of the populace than the individual congressional districts, when clear departure occurs between the House and the Senate over populist interests and special interests, the differing viewpoints in the debate will be clear, and the Senators will be left responsible to reason with the people for a greater understanding to reach an agreeable compromise that will be recognized by future generations of representatives.

By clearly defining the composure of the two different bodies of representation that more clearly delineates the natural fault lines of faction that occur within society, we will have conversations that are more honest on the issues. Likewise, the solutions offered will be more realistic and agreeable to everyone. I also believe that the natural authority the House of Representatives will have in its role as grand union on any number of popular issues will allow the House to render well-understood compromises that will bear the weight of the good-faith understanding of the American people. Business will finally have an atmosphere in which bargains can be struck with the American people themselves in a far more authoritative manner than before. This will give us a competitive advantage the rest of the world will drool over. If the huge amount of energy the average American spends worrying about her or his security is channeled into good-faith solutions that work for everyone and raise productivity and capability in the process, we will all quickly be awash in surplus.

8. Make those responsible for bringing charges against individuals in public office more directly accountable to their electorate.

Bureaucracy is currently not held accountable. Investigations are not conducted. The entire process of accountability has been politicized. Due to the control money has over the modern political process, accountability doesn't exist. Let me say that again. We have no accountability, and we must have it! We will fail as a nation if we do not. It is a matter of national security. The peace of this nation, and quite frankly the world, depend on it!

9. Force the issue of educating the populace in civics and their political civic duty.

Currently, many Americans have very little understanding of the political process or what their personal responsibilities are. They are losing hope as their votes continue to make very little difference in the law-making process. By changing the system to reflect the reality that ownership in the American government is inescapable, we also underscore the reality that preparation for this ownership is equally inescapable. Forcing the issue of needing to educate the electorate to serve as possible Congressmen and Congresswomen in the public process should start the long overdue task of thoroughly analyzing our citizenship requirements and various confederate systems of education to ensure that an educated populace (which is widely recognized as the one crucial ingredient to a working republic) becomes and remains our primary focus.

10. Restore some shred of dignity to the United States Congress.

We have all seen the approval ratings. This point stands for itself. The current process ensures that the few individuals performing the role of public servant with good intent can be overwhelmed by any number of peers on the take. Let's assume it's not their fault and treat them like addicts that need to be saved from themselves. I am sure they will argue greed and the importance of the current campaign finance system. Then they will offer compromise on the amount of money that can go into the campaigns, or offer more limits to some of the types of PACs and maybe reign in the super PACs. These are all meaningless gestures, tantamount to the promises alcoholics would make to explain how they will control their drinking and why their continued addiction is functionally necessary. I am suggesting a cold-turkey approach. We need sobriety of the first order in the House of Representatives, and money is the drug of choice that has been impeding their judgment. The use has gotten out of control.

Upon adoption of the proposed amendment, nothing initially changes. In the next election that takes place, we decide who leaves and who stays. As new members of the Congress are added, the old guard will be necessary to explain the unwritten and unspoken traditions and agreements that are a natural part of the ongoing business of our politics, and they'll aid in the transition and change that an entirely new environment of accountability will involve. We may decide it best to clean house all at once, but I highly doubt it! I expect that once the parties realize losing a seat in the House of Representatives means losing a seat they have no reliable way of gaining back, because party loyalty usually means far more than they would ever espouse to the rest of us, they will all become very agreeable to listening to their constituents' needs and concerns. In fact, I expect an explosive, newfound fervor for the people from both sides of the aisle, out of sheer fear for survival. How many of us have had to react when our jobs were at stake due to a game-changing paradigm shift within the industry, and we were in fear of not being able to pay the mortgage? Certainly as more members are replaced through the pool selection process, the overall composure of the House will be mostly individuals who are so moderate in their overall views that they would fail to be defined readily by today's Republican or Democratic parties. I think that fact alone will go a long way toward casting a tall shadow of common sense in the midst of the political machinery, next to which the ridiculous portions of both existing parties will look all the more remarkably inappropriate to the American people. I believe that the Senate, the executive branch, and both political parties will become incrementally more representative of the American populace as a natural result of a House of Representatives that is more representative of the American populace!

11. Prevent violence, bloodshed, and mass protest.

The 99 percent are not incorrect in the knowledge that they have been sold out for quite some time. Politics has clearly favored the accumulation of capital to an extreme fault. The current political system is weighted to represent dollars, not people. My proposed amendment will allow the 99 percent a more meaningful seat of power in the law-making process through peaceful means.

Every lesson history has taught me on the subject of a disproportionate distribution of wealth involves a lot of death! It very often does not go well for the rich. It never goes well for the poor. I am not going to dwell on various endgame scenarios along these lines, because I consider them to be the result of erroneous thinking to begin with. Overall human wealth and capability is not a zero-sum game. We can work together to figure out a compromise where everyone is far better off than the current future allows. This, after all, is the proud heritage of our nation!

12. Model success to the world.

During the Arab Spring and post–Saddam Hussein Iraq, if the power had been evenly distributed among the populace in a way that could not be slowly usurped, those governments would have had a far better chance of succeeding. The current state of our government is not working, and we have a growing population of discontented poor as the wealth disparity increases to historical highs. At the same time, our government is allowing money to influence the political process more than ever. Any system that models itself on the current state of affairs is doomed.

I want our form of government to be the envy of the world! At the very least, it should control minority faction of the wealthy and powerful, if we are to ever offer it as a template for a solution to a struggling people in any part of the world. In other parts of the world, the rich and powerful are not nice and enlightened like ours. Trust me on this!

A Quick Note Regarding the Wealthy

I do want us all to take a moment to thank the rich and powerful of our nation for not being evil, maniacal monsters. If they were, our problems would be much clearer—and horribly different in their manifestation. I understand that they are as unhappy as I am with the complete lack of accountability in our government and the expense it bears, with results none of us are happy to pay for. I understand that their grip on political power is out of the same fears of stability and personal survival in an ever-changing world as our individual fears of powerlessness. My goal is not to demonize the wealthy. That would be stupid. The current dysfunction I describe does exist, however, and the implications are real. I trust that the wealthy will see the benefit of the solution I offer and realize what a loss a distrust in "the casino" would have on the future of gaming in this town.

The ability to ensure that a cross-section of the average population can maintain its hold on government has never been an easy task. In today's age, in most places, they are at such an extreme disadvantage to external as well as internal economic and political forces, with no advantage of geographical isolation or protection, that the aspect of random selection might prove to be indispensable in ensuring a stable society that can house peoples of differing cultural values. If we are honest with ourselves, we will note that for the most part, it does appear we have set up dictatorships and support "royal families" who are friendly to American capitalistic ideals first, paying little concern to the life, liberty, and pursuit of happiness of the population. I don't know about the rest of you, but I refuse to be a hypocrite in the eyes of the world! It is costing us dearly. We can hardly advocate for the people of other countries to overturn systems of oppression if the only model we can offer as a replacement fails to guarantee the safety and liberties of its people. Other countries rightly see us as simply another nation ruled by tyrants, with little to offer other than possibly some help overthrowing the current tyrant in power in their neighborhood. This is the type of situation that might be good for contractors and pirates, but not much else.

In short, to prevent entire populations of other countries from running away from insolvable governments, we must work to present sustainable solutions that will work anywhere! A governmental system must be able to reliably prevent minority faction, even in places where the power is already incredibly unevenly distributed, either through property or natural abilities. I firmly believe that the core features of the Take the House Amendment could be crucial in helping to meet that need. If the rest of the world sees us adopt the change I am proposing, and if it produces significant positive change with regard to the objectives I have listed, I expect the rest of the world will take note. If we have remarkable success, it will speak well for all of Western civilization and will soundly prove to their people that a free people with a republican form of government and capitalist ideals can demand accountability and effectively control their system of government. By doing so *peacefully*, we become the envy of people of *every* nation, stated or not. If our friends across the pond, Great Britain, apply the same principals to their House of Commons, we may once again find ourselves as leading examples, prompting similar global revolution in the advance of freedom and liberty. Right now several foreign leaders are laughing at us, and they are correct to do so. This changes all of that. This would make them eat their words.

13. Introduce effective systemic change, while ensuring all functional institutions remain completely intact at current capacity, ensuring continuity and stability.

This last objective is of the utmost importance. The growing frustration of the majority of Americans who feel betrayed by their countrymen over the last few decades is at a critical level. For decades, we have been given promises that more often than not only serve further insult. Our most recent popular president, Obama, was elected simply on the campaign platform of hope for something different. Trump's only popularity is due to the statement of disgust he sends to the political machinery. Americans are at a point where many would be willing to take the dangerous and misleading advice to destroy the whole system so that we can rebuild it. I think I need to offer some insight into why anyone would offer that sort of advice. First, it would be a wonderful way to cause chaos within the government itself to allow for, chiefly, the complete destruction of any evidence of wrongdoing that the American people currently know nothing about! In addition, for those who fear that losing power may be inevitable, it would take what was a government so effective that it could suppress the population for decades and make it immediately ineffective to meet minimal needs. That, my friends, would be a terrible mistake. Second, and far more dangerous, would be to rely on the current power structure to completely rewrite all of the rules they find inconvenient and give themselves the authority to enforce whatever they want.

Fortunately, none of this nonsense is necessary. No one can argue that the republic we have established, paired with regulated capitalism, is not still the ideal structural form of government suitable to managing this nation's business. No one can pretend to offer any reasonable alternative form of government that begins to promise by design, much less display, an ability to preserve and protect along with the individual the individual's rights and freedoms of belief, expression, and self-determination, a chosen way of life, or simply the right to be alive.

Because the passing of the Take the House Amendment would not remove the current sitting House members immediately, there would not be a complete brain-drain. In an effort to maintain their traditional hold on the roles of the House, the two parties would attempt to work together to pass meaningful legislation. I would expect existing House members to offer solutions and legislation like never before, because they realize that they are now being held accountable to serve all of the American people. As new members are voted into the House, the flaws in the current two-party division will become apparent, and a natural transition will occur as the parties themselves change to reflect the more rational and centrist views of the new Congress. For the first time, we might see something actually trickle down in a good way, as the new attitude of the parties that emerge will recognize their common ground as sacred, distilling that attitude to all offices still affected by partisan influence. The flow of the business remains the same. However, over a short amount of time, it will be done by people who look like, and in all actuality more directly represent, all of us.

Frankly, I don't expect the two-party system to last in its current form. With random selection of replacements, even if the American people did want to get rid of an entire party, we wouldn't have to worry about the usual repercussions associated with handing the whole balance of power over to another party that has sold different souls to different devils. Let me say that again, because it has been a limit in the game theory of our current legislative system. We could remove an entire offending party from power in the House of Representatives without major concern of the other parties being handed all of the power! I expect this reality to sink in fast and to have some very real therapeutic benefits to those within the various party leadership positions today. Once they know that their place in the House of Representatives is earned by the American people, and that there is nothing to prevent their complete removal, they can focus on being an aid to the representative in forming legislation, by lobbying their values and interests on the matter. The parties will have to actually identify what values they stand for, communicate them clearly to the American people as well as the representatives, and figure out how those claimed values apply to the legislative and administrative tasks before our representatives. This is a big change from the type of team sport both major parties have been playing. One would think the parties will benefit greatly from freeing themselves from this ridiculous, cartoonish political wrestling match that our politics has become. Both parties will know that we can safely remove them with no ill effect. The American people will do just fine.

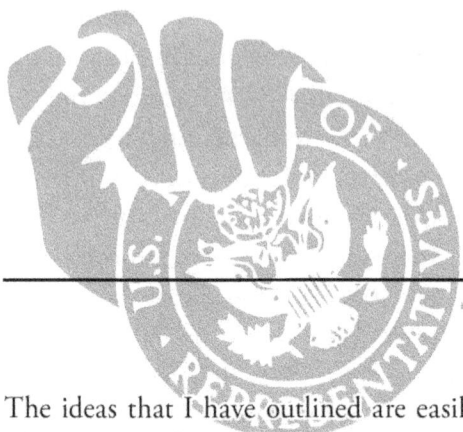

Tactics

The ideas that I have outlined are easily achievable. In the last decade, I have seen political fury and outrage that have grown in strength and momentum. Without a healthy target on which to focus that anger, we risk lashing out at one another—or worse, being successfully divided on issues that are symptoms of problems instead of identifying the core issues that affect us and then doing something about them. The tactic of getting us to fight among ourselves in order to ignore a real threat is as old as humanity itself. It is called divide and conquer, and it has been if full force over the last several decades in order to get the lower classes to spend enough energy fighting over social issues that the ruling class can steal from them, lie to them, cheat them, rob them, deny them political power, deny them property, deny them access to schooling, and deny them access to clean drinking water. We can get both sides to fight about abortion—while no one works on the issue of what to do with unwanted children. We can get both sides to argue about marriage equality—while no one ponders the fact that the only lesson we are learning as a whole about marriage is that roughly half of us will give up on a commitment to another individual, usually teaching the second hard lesson to the children in the situation: they are unwanted and were a mistake. The world didn't have any plans for them, and the institution that brought them into the world was never really serious or has changed its collective mind.

I could give endless examples, but embarking on that journey only serves to empower further confusion on the issue at hand, and there is only one core issue at hand: we need a system that prevents our public servants from selling out large portions of the American population.

This can be done, but it is going to take solidarity in vision and focus that we, as a people, have not had in quite some time. Our enemy is not a foreign power or any single anti-American (or even anti-capitalistic) worldview. Our enemy is ourselves. Our current situation is a direct reflection of the values we have abandoned as individuals in our most basic relationships. It is the result of placing personal greed over the well-being of those around us. It is characterized by resentment at the burdens we have to carry for others. It expresses frustration with the kind of patience and understanding it takes to invest in others to ensure continuity of anything meaningful. It exposes no collective plan or preparation for a future that can accommodate all of us.

UNDERSTAND CHANGE TO THE CONSTITUTION

Many of us have no clue what is in the constitution, much less how any of it actually works, including the amendment process. We may be of the opinion that this is too hard to accomplish. I assure you it is not. Take some time to do a little research on the institution you are being called to take ownership of, and hope that the Internet reports an uptick in our collective curiosity on the matter!

Calling for a change to the constitution can be done in one of two ways. The first involves the US House of Representatives and the US Senate. The bill containing the amendment would need to pass both of these legislatures with a two-thirds majority vote. This is the process we have used throughout our short history, with great success, to bring about necessary change to our republic.

The second method involves the state legislatures calling for a constitutional convention. This method seems more appropriate for cases where a complete breakdown of the system has occurred or is imminently evident, and entirely new proposals have to be debated, considered, explained, and adopted. The very first conventions were not unlike this process, and this option exists out of doomsday necessity. I do not believe we are anywhere near this scenario yet and would hold anyone suggesting this route with great "no-fly list" suspicion.

Regardless of the means used to propose the constitutional amendment, it then goes on to the various legislatures of the fifty states. Three-quarters of the state legislatures need to ratify the amendment for it to become a part of the constitution.

It is interesting to note that the president has no part in this process. The president is effectively a bystander while the American corporate board at the federal and regional levels figures out what the new corporate rules will be. Personally, I am relieved at this, considering how dubious the current president's mandate will be over the next four years. Having covered the strategy of avoiding the judiciary with this particular course of action, we are left only needing to convince our representatives to perform clearly prescribed actions on an already well-defined matter.

This means that support for the amendment must happen not only at the federal level but at the state and local levels as well, and rightly so. The chief reason for such a seemingly simple amendment is that it is small enough to make a single issue. It is not complicated at all. Although deceptively simple, it is powerful, durable, and elegant in its effects.

BECOME SINGLE-ISSUE VOTERS

The question is, how do we get a broken system to adopt a constitutional amendment of this nature? Follow in the footsteps of Grover Norquist. For those familiar with American politics, Grover Norquist is a political activist who has used the tool of making "single-issue voters" powerful through his Americans for Tax Reform pledge. For almost thirty years, he has been successful in using this type of inescapable political power play to ensure raising taxes does not happen. That tactic has been extremely successful—I would argue, to the detriment of rational problem solving. Because this simple tool worked so wonderfully well to strong-arm our politicians, who were either fully in agreement with the policy or such weak, spineless, pathetic, or outright incompetent leaders that they couldn't see one logical step up into the social machinery to analyze the obvious consequences of their actions, I suggest that we, the American people, apply the same basic tactic with even more force and vigor. The only way we can secure our rights as co-owners in the American enterprise is to demand and take control of it. I am strongly of the opinion that only then will we have a legislature that can rightfully claim its authority and from which we will have authority to rationally and thoroughly correct any other number of broken and unaccountable systems that have evaded appropriate oversight. Only then will we have a system of government that is trusted by the people to be a tool of growth, instead of a tool of restraint. Only then can we figure out fair-trade laws and immigration policy and truly appreciate, within the legislature itself, the myriad concerns that need the utilities of government but are not being addressed. Only then will the appropriate people be at the table to decide on most of the other matters before us. We will finally be able to take ourselves seriously when we look one another in the eye and say, "There are some things money can't buy." I propose that this issue be seen as the nonpartisan single issue of business that must be addressed fully before any other serious matter can be effectively decided. To do that, I propose the following platform for all elections going forward until our objective is met.

> Every politician running for any public office, federal, state, county, or city (frankly, anywhere one is attempted to assign Republican or Democrat to one's name) should be forced to state whether they stand for or against the "Take the House" Amendment.

This is nothing new. We compile a database of all candidates running for office and make their stances known. If they are not for the adoption and ratification of the amendment, we don't elect them to public office at any level. If both Republicans and Democrats wish to take a stance against the amendment I am proposing, we simply create a third party with the sole focus of being the "Take the House" reform candidate. We will advertise what names to write in for each and every position at every level. It will force politicians in Washington, your state, your county, and your town to acknowledge the proposed solution, take a stance on it, and at the very least conduct themselves in a manner that realizes there are enormous, grave, and inescapable consequences for their individual and collective action and inaction.

I also think this process would be therapeutically beneficial for the American people at large, at a time when some considerable group therapy is needed. Organizing and holding politicians at all levels of all parties accountable on this one issue would be incredibly empowering to a nation of people who are sick of being marginalized. We would get to force ourselves at the local, county, state, and federal levels to recognize that the sole role and duty of the public servant at any level of governance is to serve the public. We are not asking for much. In software and systems engineering terms, we are simply calling out for a systemic refactor to more closely meet the mission statements and general specifications" listed by our founding documents, which the implementation of the system, defined in the constitution, was meant to satisfy through its instantiation! In other words, we are asking for a government that embodies the same principles with regard to a healthy representation of the populace that the people of this world have been crying out for, and striving toward, since the dawn of mankind. Ultimately, in the case of America, we simply need to live up to our own words!

The American government is our company. If you are an American citizen, you are a full owner! You have the right to access and control over the board. You have the right to demand that monetary influence, imparted in any way (unique to them statistically) to the controlling board member or relatives or business interests, is seen as corruption, which should be a federal "wear orange and shower with the general population of your fellow Americans for ten-to-fifteen years" offense! The person offering the bribe should be seen as an enemy of the state who is attempting to subvert the political process. In terms of rights, it's that simple. This doesn't need a new party. This doesn't cry out for a new government. It doesn't call out for creative destruction in any way. It is completely in line with our stated values and goals as a people. It is peaceful. It assumes the best in us and demands that we, as individuals and as a nation, take personal, focused action to once again rise to the occasion. It is entirely rational, possible, and likely. It is a prime example of order for order's sake during a process in which extreme complexity must be manageable!

TRACK PROGRESS AND BE RELENTLESS

Tracking support for this single issue is incredibly simple compared to just about any other means of change we might attempt. It should enable us to focus clearly on which federal, state, and local officials can be relied on to operate the mechanics of the legislative and ratification processes that need to take place. The single issue we are focusing on—essentially, the right to fair representation in the legislature—is of the utmost importance! This is not an issue that can or should be kicked down the road for a few years. If, after reading about the Take the House Amendment, the American public agrees with its necessity, we should demand it be enacted before attempting any other serious legislation. Support and progress will be so easy to track that I believe we will have no problem moving swiftly forward, with what should, by any estimation, be a relatively seamless transition. Let everyone currently serving in the role of public servant know we are serious! Let them know they will be replaced, but we will not. Let them know that many Americans have sacrificed themselves in very real terms for their country, and that the current House member's symbolic gesture of sacrifice in supporting this measure is precisely what is needed at this juncture. They can take solace in knowing that proponents currently sitting in the House will probably not be voted out of office. We can let them know that we've got their backs in reforming the system to something where the "good guys" can win in the legislature too! We can track our progress on this together and know exactly where to focus in order to reach our goal. We have already planned the work; now we simply need to work the plan.

ESTABLISH INTEGRITY IN THE CONGRESS

There are a number of difficult problems we need to address, as well as compromises we need to make as a nation. Once our government's composure is reflective of our citizenry, only then will we be able to render solutions of authority that we can all have faith in. I am not interested in any partisan speculation about where legislation may lead after this change. I am interested only in maintenance to the machinery of the infrastructure at this point in time. However, there is one more immediate change that I think will be crucial to address right away, if an atmosphere of reliable accountability is to be established within the legislature. I believe that getting the House of Representatives to accept the following code of conduct is essential to a healthy legislative branch. I also believe that the current members of the House are incapable of demanding this from themselves. If this is the first order of business within the new House of Representatives, an alert electorate will be able to quickly identify and prune out those who have numerous reasons explaining why being held to a code of complete honesty is "problematic." Getting rid of these highly deceptive individuals, regardless of party affiliation, is necessary for the health of the legislature, and it's good for the existing parties themselves.

Honor Code

As I have stated before, the public education I received growing up was one of the best primary and secondary educational opportunities in the world. It prepared me very well academically for the rigor of the program at the Air Force Academy. I mentioned the honor code that was observed and enforced by the student body: "We will not lie, steal or cheat, nor tolerate among us anyone who does." This honor code was considered nonnegotiable. Officers entrusted with the role of safeguarding our nation and its arsenal do not have the right or the luxury of allowing an atmosphere of corruption to exist; the stakes are simply too high. We can lose trust in every office of the land, but if we lose faith in those actually tasked with being the final physical safeguard to our existence from ourselves and others, we are past a critical point of no return. Everyone agrees with this policy. No one in his right mind would pretend to voice otherwise to the American public.

The armed forces are not perfect, and they are reliant on private and public industry. Like any agency of humanity, the armed forces demand external oversight to ensure that individuals and corporations are not taking advantage of a system that cannot always manage its own purse strings. Senior officers do end up looking for a place to land after they have completed their military careers. The same tendencies toward corruption and relationships of obviously conflicting (and often completely inappropriate) interests exist in this organization just as they do in the federal reserve, justice department, and the legislature. With so many boundaries where conflicts of interest can occur, it would be reasonable to assume that the House of Representatives, tasked with oversight and accountability of the military and the various other institutions vital to the ongoing stability and security of our people and our society, would be held to at least as high a standard of integrity as the men and women whom they appoint and commission. Instead, much like the general who gives juicy contracts to buddies in the defense industry he or she wishes to soon work for, in order to become a Congressperson, you have to take morally questionable sums of money as a precursor. Politicians go into the job owing loyalties first to unknown persons. They are tainted and untrustworthy by nature. The current approval rating of the Congress, which I will safely assume is still ridiculously low, is where it should be. How could the American people trust an institution that operates no differently in its business model than prostitution?

One of the key benefits of the Take the House Amendment is the ability to completely remove the necessity for any campaign finance. It allows us to set new ground rules for what will be allowable behavior from our public servants who stand accountable for the most vulnerable within our society, and in whom we entrust our liberties. It would be entirely reasonable to apply the honor code to our Congressmen and Congresswomen. We have a good model for it, and it works. It would also be entirely reasonable to swear them in whenever conducting official business, because they should naturally consider themselves as on the record during the entire tenure of their office. They should be well aware that in positions of great power and responsibility, the consequences for betraying the trust of the American people do not decrease—they increase exponentially! When politicians deceive the American people, they threaten the fabric of the social trust that binds us together as a people. They threaten our safety and security in the same fundamental manner as a terrorist's bomb blast.

It is important to note that we have had to accept our government explaining to us that we live in a post-9/11 world and that liberties we used to take for granted were illegally trampled over for our own good. We were naive. Things are different. There's no need to actually address the erosion of liberty at its most fundamental level.

There is a problem with this thinking. The government has the ability to quite literally see and hear everything we are doing and saying to one another. They can track everyone we come into contact with, keep perfect records of all of it for as long as they want, and use sophisticated technologies to manipulate society as a result in ways we have no way to find out about. This group of people contains a cohort that has a long and consistent track record of abusing every loophole they can get their hands on to the detriment of the American people as a whole. The conversation of what else must change in order to maintain a stable government and a free society, given these new capabilities and requirements, has yet to occur in the public arena. I would argue that the only arrangement where this new normal is tenable is one where we, as the owners of the House of Representatives, can demand the truth as a matter of fact from our Congress, or they are immediately replaced by lottery! This is far from an unreasonable standard.

Accountability has to start somewhere, and the stakes have never been higher. Enforcing an honor code within the House of Representatives is a reasonable minimum standard to demand. Doing so would solve the vast majority of the issues of corruption, fraud, distrust, and despair that infests our current system and the individuals operating within it. If you plan on serving your nation in the capacity of a legislator, then you must examine your own ability to be truthful at all times regarding every aspect of your conduct. You should be prepared to have nothing to hide, because the American people can afford your secrets far less than the American government can afford the average citizen's right to privacy. Accountability starts at the top—there is no other way! An extreme amount of trust has been lost in what is such a vital instrument of our combined security. A measure of zero tolerance in the application of an honor code is the correction that is required to return the balance to equity.

EDUCATE THE PEOPLE

The Civics Lesson

I remember my first day of civics class in high school. I was a year younger than most of the kids in the class. Civics was one of those required classes that acted as a filler in the scheduling system, so having a mix of ages wasn't uncommon. I don't remember the name of the man at the front of the class. He looked as though the experience of teaching over two decades of teenagers from a small Wisconsin town had treated him hard, and there was very little humor in his eyes. Eventually, the class settled down and became quiet. When they had, he proceeded to give the following speech. This is not word for word, but it is close. I have tried to stay true to its intent, but I will confess that the message may have been altered slightly over the course of my memory.

Some of you will go on to do great things. Some of you will graduate from this school and go off and do amazing things—invent new things, start new businesses. The world is your oyster. Most of you will graduate from this school, maybe go to college, maybe not, and go happily through your lives. You'll work a job for thirty to forty-five years, raise families, and retire. That's fine. Some of you won't amount to anything. You'll drop out and go off to "find your own way." Eventually you'll grow up—or not.

That doesn't matter to me. Regardless of what you do here, what you do after here, or what your plans are, when you all turn eighteen, you have one job to do! You have to vote correctly! That means knowing how your city government works, how your state government works, and how the federal government works—what positions you vote for, and what those positions do. Listen up, because this is important stuff! When you become an adult, even if you didn't graduate from high school, you have an important job to do, and it requires that you learn some things first. I'm here to make sure you don't screw it up for the rest of us!

I will never forget what this teacher said and the impact of what he communicated. It was one of the most honest things I had ever heard out of any person up to that point in my life. It was certainly the first time someone other than my father had dropped all pretense and addressed me as an adult in training. I knew at that point in time that the business of existing as a healthy community was a complicated one that required us to become educated so

that we could make wise decisions regarding the policies
and people that determine our laws and societal structure.

A lot has been said recently about the cost of education and whether
schools and teachers are performing up to standards. Thinking back on the
incredible investment my community made in the schools I went to and
of all of the problems facing us now, I see that my civics class held the root
of the answer. The material covered was not difficult. It did require some
honest discussions about boring political topics and how they affected our
lives, which admittedly were hard to appreciate at the time. I do believe a
renewed focus on civic responsibility is something crucial to continuously
promote to the existing adults, as well as the coming generations. The focus
on the INS exam as a minimal means test was not a mistake. The issue of
mass educational preparation needs to be codified and addressed. Until
we do have a more unified educational approach to teaching civic duties,
habits, principals, and values, I ask that those teaching the content today
consider the speech I was given. Please keep giving it!

My next point might force us to get uncomfortably honest with
ourselves. When I test-drive this solution with other people, the first
reaction I get is one of excitement … quickly followed by dismay. They ask,
"But have you met most people?" I respond that I have. They confirm that
their fear would be that idiots who don't know what they are doing would
be in charge. My response is always, "Do you think an idiot can pass the
INS exam?" It is a trick question, because I can safely assume 99 percent of
the time, the answer is "I don't know," and the answer is accompanied by
a sheepish admission that there is no way most of us would pass it in our
current state as citizens! This is also a structural deficiency of our republic,
and it must be corrected immediately.

The issue goes further than this. In a review of *The Forward to the Great
Conversation (Great Books of the Western World)* (*Encyclopedia Britannica*,
1957), which I read as a child, the problems identified in the 1950s and the
requisite education that we and any free people require in order to maintain
a free society is clearly identified as universal liberal arts education. It is
the education of rulers! It is the education I received as public education
necessary to the defense and preservation of the republic! If we are a free
people, and we are all expected to have the responsibilities, considerations,

and duties of rulers, then we must also have the preparation to do so! If we do this for only an elite few, only a few will be able to perform the role. None will stand prepared to judge those performing the tasks and making the rules, and the resulting society will be a dim reflection of this lack of capability. In the best-case scenario, an uneducated society will merely continue to dance on, following familiar patterns but without understanding and insight into why we conduct business within certain offices and institutions of the government, or how that business should be conducted. In this environment, corruption, tyranny, and collapse are inevitable. Knowledge is the breath that keeps society alive and healthy.

Now for the scary part of the conclusion.

If one reads through *The Forward to the Great Conversation,* one will find a warning to the West, and America specifically, about the direction we were headed in our educational focus. In the 1950s, these folks stated we were going off the rails by neglecting to teach the principles contained in the combined knowledge of our history and tradition. They stated what education would be required to dig our way out. I got that type of education. I'm offering a solution to the types of problems they were talking about, which we are facing today. I'm telling you they were correct about the need for precisely this type of education for the masses.

We the people of the United States are being judged by the world community for how we proceed. Consider at this point in time what our problems are from our perspective, and then consider our situation from any number of alternative perspectives the many nations and peoples of this world have to offer. We are on display now more than ever! If all that other nations see on the TV and movies are fat, stupid, uneducated morons, and all they see from the news media are reports of our most outrageous behavior, and statistically most of what they see of us on the Internet is not good, then they will have no pity on us when we falter. Worse yet, they will look at our wealth and leisure as vices that should be taken away so as not to "spoil the children." The case will be made that we cannot keep that which we clearly have not kept, and any notion of wasting education on people like us will be seen as doubling down on a problem too big not to fail.

I believe strongly that we must answer the hanging question the world has about what the American people have become, and whether we, not our leadership or those in power, have lost our way. We must show the world that our system of government can maintain liberty while being accountable to the American people. Let's respond to the world's question and doubt in a way that once again forces others to stand in awe and respect for our history of living up to our best words!

In proposing the Take the House Amendment, I call for securing the rights of ownership along with noting the responsibilities it entails. We need to analyze what should be required of each and every one of us in our educational understanding as citizens, with the incredible opportunity in time and space that we have to effectively manage our own affairs. The fact I am simply repeating a call made to my father's and grandfather's generation over fifty years ago that still rings true today stands as witness to a world that is still judging our performance on the same preparation criteria when it comes to the fitness of our form of republic in its ability to stand the test of time, while offering a secure and stable society for all of its people. This is the rationale behind a push towards universal education we hear from progressives such as Bernie Sanders today. What they ask for and why they feel so strongly about it should be obvious, if you have read this far. Pulling it off pragmatically is something that will take a lot of work, and like the many other complicated issues we have, it will require ongoing compromise and change. These issues are best left to a better Congress than we have today. Regardless, like establishing a basis of honor, trust, and accountability in the Congress, a proper system of education to the same ends is needed.

I dare my generation to answer that call soundly by confirming to the world that the correct preparations were taken, that the proper learning was conveyed, that the appropriate solutions were found as a result, and that future success was ensured through the establishment of ongoing educational programs and real leadership and service opportunities beyond the limited scope of our defense industry to make sure the American populace at large stands united and ready to lead by example into this new millennium.

What I Know about Americans

Given a clear understanding of the problem, a pragmatic solution that addresses all of the above issues, and a little time to consider the matter among themselves, the American people will act quickly and decisively in making the solution a reality. It makes me smile, knowing firsthand what amazing individuals of which this nation is composed. We all know it to be true, and the rest of the world knows it deep down as well. History has been faithful in confirming what we hope about ourselves: that after exhausting all other resources, we will eventually do the right thing. We have faced far more difficult, immediately dire, and complex political problems in the past, and every time we have emerged with an answer that is more correct than the last. Within our collective nature, we have no problem identifying right and wrong, and I would even go so far as to say that American individuals have no problem standing up for what is right. I would argue, as has been the case in the past, that this silent majority has been effectively identified, suppressed, denied promotion and power within their respective fields and communities, and effectively alienated. Far from having gone away, they sit waiting, saving their energy for any plan that will work. Once they have that, when they're sure of their footing, coordinated Americans execute like a machine! If they also have basic morality on their side, their victory is inevitable! Let the hope and change that we have as a people be hope in ourselves, and let the change be that which is ignited in ourselves and others as a result.

I believe so strongly in our natural inclination and abilities, due to our truly proud history as a people since we have been a nation. When you take in the good, the bad, and the ugly, we are still a people with an almost embarrassing overabundance of love and the kind of illogical mercy and allowance for freedom that can only come from certain strength. If anything, our greatest failure is too much trust in too few of us, and not enough trust in all of us. That is a good place to be, and in that spirit, I offer this solution to empower a fuller expression of "we the people" so that aspect of our nature can shine through more clearly in our collective lives.

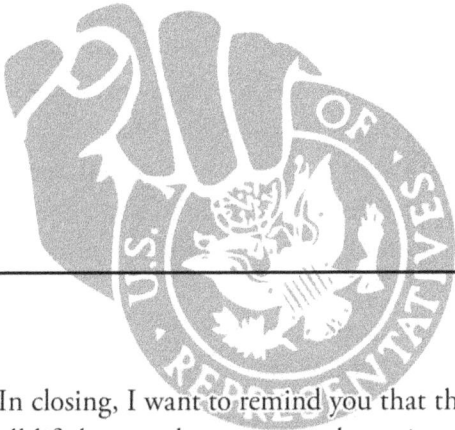

Final Remarks

In closing, I want to remind you that this work represents the product of all life has taught me across the various disciplines to which I have been exposed. It is the product of reflecting on why, even when stuck doing work that appears to have no meaning. It reflects a faithful concern over matters I was told not to worry about, matters I was told would never change, and matters no one else is addressing.

The beauty of this country is that if one of us does the homework for the class, we all get to reap the rewards. It is the spirit behind the concept of the patent system! The difficulty lies in getting the class to first realize that someone has actually attempted to do the homework assignment, and then getting them to review the work (and any competing answers) in order to judge whether it is the answer on which the class as a whole should be graded. I have done what I felt led to do, and although I am convinced that what I have laid out in the preceding pages is the most correct answer our generation can give to the problems it faces, it ultimately lies to you to be the judge of my intentions and the soundness of my logic.

I would point out that in the solution I have offered, I have nothing to gain beyond the prospects of enrichment that will be common to us all. I have identified no new specter that haunts humanity, and contrary to lifting up any one personality, party, or institution as our savior, I clearly point out (as has been done repeatedly throughout human history) the issues of continual division resulting in a societal confusion and dysfunction that allow large portions of the population to be unprotected from the actions of their fellow citizens and foreign corporate interest. My solution is nothing more than declaring that we must all take ownership of our government as the communal vehicle by which we secure our rights as individuals and establish the rule of law that determines our national societal character. Then we should recognize that we must, as a first critical priority, ensure that we are educating the full citizenry to take ownership of this institution. I see this as an evolution that has been a long time coming throughout human history. It speaks to the consistent successes all classes of our society have had in proving their place as equals in it, forcing those of us currently in power to open our eyes and increase our limited view a little more than we had in the past.

No one who is well enjoys the task of standing before history to do the work of resolving where we are at now, figuring out how we got there, and attempting to divine and engineer a path forward. In fact, I have heard similar words recently expressing that some don't believe it is necessary at this point in time. Obviously, I disagree. It is exactly what we all must do periodically. The call for education that prepares the citizenry to be capable of the critical work of historical analysis and proper social engineering of solutions was made decades ago, as I have pointed out previously. If we have a lack of voices offering solutions, we shouldn't wonder why. If we are incapable of collectively understanding appropriate solutions when they are placed in front of our faces by individuals we have no reason to distrust, we are the blind who cannot even be led.

For those of you who wonder whether the stakes are real, in early October 2016, as I was finishing the rough draft of this book, China's news agency released a scathing report highlighting our obvious dysfunction on display for the international community. They openly point out that our system of government would be an unacceptable solution for the rest of the world, and they openly mock our democratic system and the quality of our leaders. They mean to discredit us on the world stage, and the bitter reality is that they do so fairly. They claim the Western tradition to be inferior, and they call into question the legitimacy of our democratic and capitalistic society as a valid model for anyone. This is unacceptable! The solution I offer would shut them right up and give their people something to consider when they see us solve seemingly impossible problems that plague all systems of government throughout the world. And we'd do so as a free people! If we do nothing, we have nothing with which to refute their argument in the eyes of the rest of the world. I believe we have the answer, are capable of the task, and as a people are ready to take action. The time is now.

I will leave you, appropriately, with the closing of *Common Sense*. For those of you who are unfamiliar with the work, it was a letter written by one of the colonists, Thomas Paine, calling for a separation from England (meaning war), with the intent of forming a new government.

> On these grounds I rest the matter. And as no offer hath yet been made to refute the doctrine contained in the former editions of this pamphlet, it is a negative proof, that either the doctrine cannot be refuted, or, that the party in favor of it are too numerous to be opposed. WHEREFORE, instead of gazing at each other with suspicious or doubtful curiosity, let each of us hold out to his neighbor the hearty hand of friendship, and unite in drawing a line, which, like an act of oblivion, shall bury in forgetfulness every former dissension. Let the names of Whig and Tory be extinct; and let none other be heard among us, than those of a good citizen, an open and resolute friend, and a virtuous supporter of the RIGHTS of MANKIND, and of the FREE AND INDEPENDENT STATES OF AMERICA.

Acknowledgments

The excerpt from *The Federalist Papers* is taken from "Federalist No. 1," General Introduction for the *Independent Journal*, by Alexander Hamilton, at *www.congress.gov/resources/display/content/ The+Federalist+Papers#TheFederalistPapers-1.*

The quotation by Abraham Lincoln is from his Gettysburg Address, 1863, as transcribed by Nicolay, at *www.loc.gov/exhibits/gettysburg-address/ext/ trans-nicolay-copy.html.*

The excerpt from *Common Sense* by Thomas Paine is taken from *www. gutenberg.org/files/147/147-h/147-h.htm.*

www.ingramcontent.com/pod-product-compliance
Lightning Source LLC
Chambersburg PA
CBHW032016190326
41520CB00007B/498